T0089187

# If God Invented Baseball

Poems by

E. ETHELBERT MILLER

City Point Press

Copyright © 2018 by E. Ethelbert Miller
All rights reserved.
No portion of this book may be reproduced in any fashion, print, facsimile,or electronic, or by any method yet to be developed, without the express written permission of the publisher.

City Point Press
PO Box 2063
Westport CT 06880
www.citypointpress.com

Paperback ISBN: 978-1-947951-00-6
eBook ISBN: 978-1-947951-01-3

Third printing, February 2024

*Cover design by Barbara Aronica-Buck*
*Author photo © 2017 Rick Reinhard*
*Cover photo of Satchel Paige, courtesy of the Baseball Hall of Fame*

Writing was a curveball that I never saw coming.

– Larry Brown

Becoming a baseball fan means learning to absorb failure and be on a friendly footing with defeat.

– Phillip Lopate

Baseball is the greatest of American games.

– Thomas Edison

# Contents


| | |
|---|---|
| Preface | xi |
| Before Ball Four | 1 |
| If God Invented Baseball | 2 |
| The South Bronx | 3 |
| Baseball Is An Island Not A Field | 4 |
| Playing Until Dark | 5 |
| Fences | 6 |
| Juan, Willie and The Boys | 7 |
| Players | 8 |
| Judy | 9 |
| The Boys of Summer | 10 |
| The Walkoff | 11 |
| Bunting and The Art of Non-Violence | 12 |
| One Man's Fast Is Another Man's Slow | 13 |
| High School and The Intentional Walk | 15 |
| The Trade | 17 |
| Holy Water | 19 |
| War Catchers | 20 |
| The Bat Boy | 21 |
| The Second Child | 22 |

The Utility Infielder 23

The Knuckleball 25

The Throw 26

The Pitch Out 27

Crosetti 29

Bill Mazeroski Returns Home From The World Series 30

Fly Balls and Other Beautiful Things 31

Moe Berg 32

The First Man. Was Vic Power Created Before Adam? 33

Pumpsie Green 34

Jackie Robinson 36

Koufax and Me 37

Roy Campanella: January, 1958 38

Vida Blue 39

Barry Bonds 41

Japanese Flowers Bloom Inside A Baseball Bat 42

Baseball Blues 43

The 7th Inning Stretch 44

The Pitch Count 45

The Relief Pitcher Throws A Sonnet 47

Rain Delay 48

Playoffs 49

Wild Pitch 50

Ice Age After The Game 51

The Bullpen 52

Old Timer's Day 53

Baseball 55

Invention 56

Seasons 57

The Zen of Baseball 58

About the Author 59

# Preface

When I was growing up in the South Bronx baseball was the game I played across the street. It was in the playground next to P.S. 39. I lived at 938 Longwood Avenue on the second floor. A cousin Robert lived two floors above and possessed the name Dinky. He was two years older but ahead of his time. Dinky read books by Herman Khan, Isaac Asimov and Arthur C. Clarke.

He also loved Roberto Clemente, Tommy Davis and Don Drysdale. Dinky and I would play baseball together even when there was snow on the ground.

There is no future without baseball. There is no past either. My childhood memories will always embrace the New York Yankees of Bobby Richardson, Tony Kubek, Bill Skowron, Roger Maris, Mickey Mantle, Yogi Berra, Hector Lopez and Elston Howard. Yes, a line-up of remembrance.

The idea for *If God Invented Baseball* came from David Wilk. Our mutual love of the game encouraged the writing of many of these poems.

Thanks has to be given to the people responsible for bringing baseball back to our nation's capital. One should always have a romantic relationship with a sports team. I love the Washington Nationals with all the joy and heartbreak only a Cubs or Red Sox fan would understand.

I admire Dusty Baker and should have written this book with a toothpick in my mouth.

Here are poems that celebrate and interpret the game. They are for everyone who has experienced the magic released when three holy things come together: bat, ball and glove.

E. Ethelbert Miller
Blue Mountain Center, New York
July 22, 2017

# Before Ball Four

It was the summer
we wanted our caps
to fall from our heads.

I stood on line
outside Yankee Stadium
waiting for Jim Bouton
to sign my glove.

Bouton was a pitcher
not a writer then. I was a kid
who wanted to be a ball player.

It was years before
I knew the difference
between writing and throwing
or pitching and publishing.

# If God Invented Baseball

If God invented baseball
There would be no stealing
no balks, no wild pitches or intentional
walks. There would be no pitch-outs,
foul balls or errors. There would be
no one-hand catches or bean balls.
There would be no curves or sliders,
no rundowns, or warning tracks.

If God invented baseball there would
be no night games, no balls getting lost
in the sun. There would be no bunting
or swinging for the fences. There would
be no double plays or triple plays.

If God invented baseball
he would not rest on the seventh day.
Instead he would turn to us and say
"let's play two." He would let us bat
first while his angels danced
in the outfield.

# The South Bronx

We lived in the land of broomsticks
stickball played between cars
manholes for bases

We ran pass fire hydrants
and caught balls near curbs

Now and then someone smacked
a Spaldeen to a rooftop-

Making pigeons fly

# Baseball Is An Island Not A Field

(for Martín Espada)

No one mentioned the Dominican Republic
when I was growing up. We were all Puerto
Ricans. We were little baby bulls like Orlando
Cepeda.

# Playing Until Dark

When we could no longer see
the ball we walked home sadly
dragging our bats and sometimes
wearing our gloves on our heads.
Exhausted but happy.
The light in our eyes
even stars could see.

# Fences

In the playgrounds

there were few left-handed

hitters so right field

is where the big kids placed us.

We became ghosts of the game.

We stood alone in sunlight.

Sometimes during a third out

we escaped through a hole in the fence.

We returned home like players sent down

to the minors.

# Juan, Willie and The Boys

In the park we high-kicked
before throwing the ball.
We wanted to be Marichal
more than Mays – unless
we were running around
the bases. Then we wanted
our caps to fly off giving us
the speed the big boys
didn't have. Reaching home
we were safe.
The backs of our arms
covered with dust. Our good
shirts torn but everyone laughing —
fall down silly.

# Players

When Mickey Mantle died
I saw myself once again
jumping against a fence
in the South Bronx, the ball
coming to rest in my glove.
My own centerfield as large
as the housing projects
so many could not escape.

# Judy

From 4th to 6th grade
The back corners of my school
desks were filled with love notes
from Judy.

We practiced penmanship
as much as we played catch.

Judy was my first love
and we were married to baseball
even if we were too young to go
steady.

Judy was Chinese. After our first
kiss we traded gloves.

# The Boys of Summer

Carlton, Patrick and I
are waiting for autographs
outside Yankee Stadium. The summer
of 1960 and Mazeroski has not hit
the home run which will break our
hearts. We are years away from
memories of our wives and our children.
On this day we see Mickey Mantle coming
to work, his uniform of stripes waiting
inside. We run to catch "The Mick" to
have him sign his name on whatever we
own. Our lives sheltered from segregation.
Our mothers talking about Jackie Robinson
and how Willie Mays learned to catch a ball
while turning his back, running full speed
as if he were Emmett Till.

# The Walkoff

Our games ended
when the ball was lost.
Now and then a hit over a fence
rolled down the street into the sewer.
We blamed each other and ourselves.
We were kids caught in a playground
pushing our imaginations
to imagine ballparks.

This was years before last inning
heroics and bat flips. Men now paint
with wood, standing back admiring
the flight of their art. What is
the difference between a fence
and a frame?

# Bunting and The Art of Non-Violence

All your life you played small ball.
In elementary school you held the door
open for your teacher. This taught you
the art of bunting and kind manners.

You sacrificed being first so someone
could reach second. Once returning
to the dugout Gandhi slapped your butt
and said "good job."

He also said "the bat is not a club."

# One Man's Fast Is Another Man's Slow

Since I never learned to drive

I never called my legs wheels.

During my Bronx days

I was fast. I could catch. I could hit.

I could run.

I was captain. I could pick

My team. No slow boys. No

Over eaters.

I wanted legs like Luis Aparicio,

Willie Davis, Maury Wills

And Lou Brock.

Oh, let me write words from another book

Pinch hit and walk off the page.

Let them mention Ricky Henderson.

*Everything comes down to balls and strikes.*
*You don't need religion or God to understand this.*
*One can keep a scorecard just like God. Now and then you*
*try to slow things down by stepping out of the box.*
*I like how good hitters step back, adjust their uniforms,*
*stroke their bats, survey the field, spit, grab themselves*
*between the legs, step back into the box, touch their*
*caps, stare at the pitcher, swing the bat a few times,*
*and maybe if you're Rickey Henderson, step back out*
*of the box and do it all over again.*

# High School and The Intentional Walk

My guidance counselor
Sits behind a desk with catalogs
and big books. Her office is near
the bathroom and the broom
closet where the custodian
keeps his clean clothes and lunch.

Going to see the counselor
is worse than being sent to the main
office. In the office the old women
wear short skirts and still smile.
The guidance counselor has never
guided her face to a smile. She
is as serious as bad cafeteria food
on a Monday.

Today she wants to know
what I plan to do with my life.
She asks if I've selected a career.

She keeps asking me what I want
to do with my life. She asks if I've
selected a career. I keep listening
to her the way a manager talks
to a starting pitcher before removing him
from a game. I'm nodding and he's nodding
and I'm not listening.

My guidance counselor
extends her hand letting me know
our meeting is over. I notice her desk
sits in the middle of the room like a mound.
There is nothing but emptiness behind
every decision we make in life.

Yes, maybe I'm throwing my life away.
Maybe she's trying too hard to help.
All I know is that I'm walking out the door
and I'm out of control. I can't read the signs
anymore. I'm a high school kid knowing
I'll never see the majors or Japan.

# The Trade

Your parents call you
into their bedroom. They've
been whispering and your ears
want to hear what they hear but you
fear what it might be. Your mom
speaks first because your dad always
speaks second. You fear they both
are trying to teach you how to chew
your food, wash your hands, tuck
your shirt and tie your shoes.

Everything is unexpected like a baseball
trade. Your mom says you're going
to a new school and it's the one across
town, the place where the white kids are.
You look down at your skin and notice
for the first time you're black. You never
wore a different uniform. You've been black
all your life. You wouldn't change this for all
the blackness in the world. You wouldn't change

it for all the whiteness now.

You give your mom a Curt Flood look

and your dad nothing at all. You turn

from the doorway and walk back

to your room. You feel traded. You feel

betrayed.

Outside your window

the birds are chirping blues.

Ma Rainey is singing about the Mississippi risin'.

Sam Cooke calls from next door and says

"Yes, a flood is comin' and a change is gonna

come."

# Holy Water

It's raining today and nothing else matters.

When I was an altar boy I wanted to be Clete Boyer.

I lived on Longwood Avenue in the Bronx.

The hot corner was Kelly Street and it was hell hot.

Yankee Stadium was heaven.

Nothing more beautiful than Boyer

throwing a runner out from his knees.

# War Catchers

Once only catchers wore
their caps backwards.
Was the face mask an
introduction to prison?
You either wanted to catch
or you didn't. Catchers
walked around with bruises
and scars. Many were short
and tough. They were
veterans who sat on the bench
and told war stories about
extra inning games and no-hit
gems. Catchers turned their
caps backwards while slow-
walking to the plate. They
nodded to umpires and spoke
only to the game.

# The Bat Boy

The sound of ball against bone
was still in my head when I went
to get Gil McDougald's bat.
The park as silent as a cemetery.
The body of Herb Score cut down
at the mound and lying limp –
did the world end on May 7, 1957?

It was the day McDougald vowed
to never play again if Score lost
his right eye. I told my mom
that night I didn't want to see
another bat or ball. I had a fear
of seeing blindness and knowing
stars could disappear.

# The Second Child

(for Nyere-Gibran)

in sports they say it's difficult
to repeat, to win, to gain a championship
two consecutive years; so it is with children,
the difference, the new season, the second child.

Each beginning finds a newborn, a rookie
struggling to learn the lessons of spring,
a time of hope and expectations, of fingers
gripping and pulling things to mouth.

# The Utility Infielder

My wife without telling me
moves my books out of the basement.

I'm Tony Kubek watching the ball
take a bad bounce as it grabs my throat.
It's the 7th game of the World Series –
Yankees against Pirates.

In 1960 my wife had yet to speak
to me. We didn't even know each other.
Did Joe DeMaestri ever date or just play
every position?

I am Tony Kubek
unable to explain my life.
Long ago it was DeMaestri's baseball card
I wanted to give away. What worth
would it ever have?

Marriage is the sweet pink chewing gum
that comes with the cards. It loses
its taste before we blow and pop
that first bubble, before we divorce
or try to outrun the errors of our love.

# The Knuckleball

Every black man should be born
with a big mitt.
How else can one catch the world
that flutters in unpredictable ways.

The sound of a knuckleball
is Parker on his horn.
When Ella scats don't try
to copy her.

Oriole Hoyt Wilhelm in 1958 threw
a no-hitter against the Yankees.
It was like Douglass being Lincoln
for a day. It's impossible to dance
to slavery anymore. It ended with
the hangman's swing.

The knuckleball is Bebop.
Don't be baffled by its strange beauty.
Just keep hitting it with your ears.

# The Throw

Before darkness descended

Lightning came from right field.

Kaline, Clemente and Rocky Colavito

Threw like Gods.

No runner or sinner could run

Or dash to third.

The ballpark silenced by thunder

Hitting the glove.

Eyes blinded by the beauty

Of the throw.

# The Pitch Out

The ball moves
toward
the plate
like a note
played by
Ben Webster

a sound so large
you just listen
as it passes far
outside your ear

You're surprised
when the catcher
catches the ball
he wants to throw

The runner on first

stops

in his tracks

like a young jazz critic

Why run?

# Crosetti

Frank Crosetti
a gentleman in pinstripes
stands near third base.

How many heroes
will he escort home?

1932 and Ruth looks into
the Cubs dugout,
points a finger and calls
the shot.

A young Crosetti will think
of the Babe when he shakes
the hand of Roger Maris in
1961.

Baseball is a game played
by men who know the silence
of grace and the beauty of
records made to be broken.

# Bill Mazeroski Returns Home From The World Series

when i was a kid

i told my old man

that i would make a name for myself

like walter next door who had a hit

record on the radio for two weeks

and then enlisted and got himself shot

i want people to forget Eisenhower

i want them to remember my swing

the way I touched third and headed

home to every fan in the world

# Fly Balls and Other Beautiful Things

Bob Gibson came to Nat Turner in a dream.

He taught him how to freedom pitch and brush back slavery.

A cardinal is a messenger from God.

The arc of a Josh Gibson home run

Was what Harriet Tubman was told to follow.

The voices in her head constantly ran the bases.

Those of us who heard Frederick Douglass

learned to step off first base and get a lead.

He taught us how to avoid the pickoff and rundown.

His hair was filled with beautiful things.

# Moe Berg

What man doesn't have secrets?

What man doesn't wear a mask?

Every catcher hides his signs

from the man on second

and from the rest of the world.

If Moe Berg was a spy

he was our spy

protecting home.

Behind every catcher

only a lonely umpire

calling the game like God.

# The First Man. Was Vic Power Created Before Adam?

They yell "clown" from the dugout and stands.
"Showboat" is a foul word in the air like "Nigger."

I swear they should be yelling at Chief Wahoo on my
sleeve and not the Puerto Rican in me.

I ignore the taunts.
Why catch abuse with two hands?

If God invented baseball and wanted everyone
to be like him, why don't we play with two gloves?

# Pumpsie Green

Years before we decided to change
our names and name ourselves
I held your baseball card in black
hands and wondered who gave you
the name Pumpsie.

How unforgettable, as if Nat
King Cole had decided to sing your
name. You were the first black player
to play for Boston. I wondered about
the ear's loneliness when you got a
hit or the error someone made when
calling you to bunt and run.

How green was the Fenway field
before your arrival? Your name
a sign against segregation finally
finding a place in the locker room.

Pumpsie Green. What Red Sox
fan mistook your last name for
being Irish after being puzzled
by your first?

# Jackie Robinson

After baseball

his hair turned gray

as if someone had placed

a tarp over the field.

# Koufax and Me

(for Aviva)

One didn't have to be Jewish
to love Sandy Koufax. With Jackie
Robinson we learned to root for the best bums
in the world.

Equality was captured when he stole a base.

In 1957 the Dodgers left Brooklyn.
Stolen by Los Angeles.

Koufax became a star close to Hollywood.
I was amazed by what he could do with a curve
and how a girl could swing her hips.

I was a sutterer in school.
I was Willie Davis making those errors
in the 1966 World Series.

# Roy Campanella: January, 1958

Night as dark as the inside

of a catcher's mitt.

There are blows I can take

head on and never step back

from. When Jackie made the news

I knew I would have a chance

to play ball in the majors.

Ten years ago I put the number

39 on my back and tonight God

tries to steal home.

# Vida Blue

Before the band takes
the stage, backstage
everyone is waiting
for Vida Blue. You can't
play the music without
the pitcher or the bass
player.

"Mingus" someone mumbles,
scaring the cigarette smoke
in the corner. "Is he in the dugout
or the underground?"

It's 1971 and Vida Blue
is strumming the mound
for the Oakland A's. Notes
popping in and out of the catcher's
mitt and making the leather sing
like Ella, or is it Vaughan?

I once took the A train
to the park where I saw Blue
Moon Odom and Billy Strayhorn
standing outside the corner of first
and second. Ellington the manager
was looking dapper and had his arm
around a dame.

I swore the woman was
sweet divine and as royal as the Duke.
I was a heckler until the beer knocked
me down and Vida Blue caught me
lookin'.

# Barry Bonds

(for Dan Moldea)

Only Shakespeare could write my biography.
My swing was pure Picasso, surreal to the average
player and fan. Forget the Babe.
My name is Bonds. Barry Bonds.
I was blessed by the gods and my godfather
is Willie Mays. Yes, I played for the Giants
and was once a Pirate. Folks try to place a patch
over my records but it only makes them blind
to beauty. Every rumor comes with steroids
and becomes larger with every lie. Leaving
me out of the Hall of Fame makes the place
nothing but a hall. Call me the Ali of baseball.
The greatest of them all.

# Japanese Flowers Bloom Inside A Baseball Bat

Baseball is spoken

in every language.

Ichiro stretches

at bat and in the outfield.

Mariner, Yankee

Marlin.

Every hit

a haiku.

# Baseball Blues

Dusty Baker plays his toothpick like a guitar.

A bad bullpen will always give a team the baseball blues.

# The 7th Inning Stretch

(for Lynda Tredway)

Let me rise like Lazarus.

Let me bask in the sun with my fellow fans.

Let me sway with the music.

Let me point at the scoreboard and ignore the score.

Let me wave my cap.

Let me open my arms and embrace my last innings.

Let me celebrate baseball.

Let me celebrate life.

# The Pitch Count

Is it the 9th inning
when death jogs from the bullpen
to face you in your final at bat?
Or maybe it's spring training
when hope fails like health
and the team heads north
without you.

Blame it on the pitch count
when you slump after the All-Star
game in the middle season of your
life.

Suddenly the fever of August and the first
chill of September followed by knowing
you will not play in October.

There is something final

and not forgiving about the final out.

The ball taken from your hand.

Baseball begins and ends at home.

# The Relief Pitcher Throws A Sonnet

You have to forget the last election.

The blown save.

What matters is now, not tomorrow, just now.

In every inning there is the possibility of something going wrong,

the way sunlight blinds or the way a ball skips towards

the wall or through and under a glove. You stand on the mound

of your imagination and imagine nothing except your own breath.

In your hands the roundness of the world.

How do you feel? Is this what you've always wanted?

It's not about the score or getting out of the inning.

It's about saving whatever needs to be saved. It can be nothing

more than one's reputation or helping a child crave the memory

of magic and something to believe in. There is nothing more

human than baseball.

# Rain Delay

The rain stops in mid-air
like Satchel Paige throwing
his hesitation pitch or the Supreme
Court deciding it's all deliberate
speed when it comes to integration.

Segregation was America's dark cloud,
a mud stain on white uniforms.
The scoreboard a reminder that waiting
was a wasted turn at bat.

The rain continues to fall in one direction.
Who can say this is progress?

# The Playoffs

while i watch the playoffs
you use my phone to call
some other man

you stay until
the fifth inning
then you say you have
to leave

i watch you exit
like a pitcher heading
for the showers

somewhere someone
is keeping score

you perfect your game
with each man

love is the best curve
a woman can throw

# Wild Pitch

She throws the pillows to the floor

with hurt and anger. It's difficult to determine

where the plate of love is.

You want to call this home but a divorce

is as good as a walk.

# Ice Age After The Game

I remove shoes

Socks and pants.

I reach for the ice

For arms and knees.

How many blocks

Now turn into innings?

I can barely walk.

Is this intentional?

I unbutton my shirt

And stare at the gray

Splinters of hair. I place

The ice everywhere.

In this game

Nothing melts faster

Than age.

# The Bullpen

I enter the assisted
living home. Everyday
is Sunday here.

Instead of pews
many sit in wheelchairs.

Our last innings
are when we give thanks
for small things.

Elders are closers.
We turn to them for hope
as they rise and march

into history wearing
crowns, suits and shoes
that shine.

# Old Timer's Day

The workers arrived today
bringing tools to change
my home place. My place
one day will no longer be safe.
This is what aging does to
the body, when things fail
and the walls of youth become
Berlin after the cold war.
Old age is coldness, bones
reduced to everything that is
fragile. How we break is how
we suffer, it's how we die,
it's how we dream backwards.

The workers install railings
and handle bars to prevent
my falling as if falling in love
was still possible. I loved the
Yankees when I was young,

when I thought I could be
a pitcher, yes, I wanted my name
to be called on Old-Timer's Day
after all my mistakes and errors.

Call my name God after Jim Coates,
Art Ditmar, Ryne Duren, Whitey
Ford, Don Larsen, Duke Maas, Bobby
Shantz, Ralph Terry, Bob Turley,
Luis Arroyo and tall Steve Hamilton.
Call my name God when I walk
slowly from the dugout to wave
at the crowd, tip my hat and call
it a day.

# Baseball

Let me sit in the ball park
cap turned backwards and
praying for a rally. I need
the sun and sweat to remind
me how much I love the game,
how each year it comes down
to the last inning, the final out.

# Invention

Across the street Thomas Edison

listens to Bessie Smith and decides

the blues are too painful

for anyone crying alone in the dark.

# Seasons

Spring training again

Young players replace the old

The game is too short

# The Zen of Baseball

Maybe we should play baseball
by the lake. The motion of water
as still as a pitcher waiting for a sign.
The surrounding trees standing
like coaches and managers.
Who wouldn't want to walk across
the lake into immortality.

# About the Author

E. Ethelbert Miller is a writer and literary activist. He is the author of several collections of poems and two memoirs and serves as a board member for the Greater Washington Community Foundation. For fourteen years Miller has been the editor of *Poet Lore,* the oldest poetry magazine published in the United States. In April 2015, Miller was inducted into the Washington DC Hall of Fame. In 2016, he received the AWP *George Garrett Award for Outstanding Community Service in Literature* and the DC Mayor's Arts Award for *Distinguished Honor*. Miller currently serves on the faculty at the University of Houston/Victoria and hosts the weekly morning radio show *On the Margin* which airs on WPFW-FM 89.3. His most recent book is *The Collected Poems of E. Ethelbert Miller* edited by Kirsten Porter and published by Willow Books.